For Andie —
With warmest
from Hyman
November 2024

OUR MORAL LIFE
Dispelling Its Mysteries

HYMAN GROSS

Published independently in 2024

Copyright © 2024 Hyman Gross

All rights reserved.

ISBN: 9798344268750

DEDICATION

To Andie and Munizha, my perfect midwives

CONTENTS

	Introduction	1
1	What Is Our Moral Life?	6
2	Moral Consciousness	12
3	Ourselves and Others	26
4	Religion and Our Moral Life	39
5	Law and Our Moral Life	46
6	Four Moral Mischiefs	56

INTRODUCTION

Everyone knows the story of the elephant and the blind men. Each of the men feels a different part of the elephant and thinks that the whole elephant is really like the part he can feel.

But let's take this further.

Suppose the men talk to each other. It dawns on them there must be some great creature with all the things that each of them has been touching. Their sense of smell tells them something about this creature, as do the trumpeting sounds and elephant movements. The men remain without a vision of that great beast we see in the zoo, but each man does have an impression of an elephant, with his own imagined creature lodged in his mind.

Our moral life is like the elephant. Philosophers, scientists, and others investigate it from different perspectives and with different interests. Each has an idea of some aspects of our moral life, but no one has a picture of our moral life in its entirety. And there is another problem. Strangers from other parts of our life wander in and make themselves at home. Being seen as part of our moral life is something that others wish to take advantage of.

In my previous book, **Moral Mischief**, I made a start in identifying some key elements in our moral life, and went on to examine the mischief-making they give rise to. *I want in this book to make our moral life as a whole more explicit. I want to provide a picture of the whole of what in reality is being talked about when parts of our moral life are being explained and expounded*

INTRODUCTION

from different points of view. What I offer is only a sketch. It does not purport to be a picture of our moral life in all its detail, only a picture that helps us better understand that our moral life is not the simple affair it is often taken to be.

* * *

I take note first of half a dozen of these explanatory and expository enterprises that give us different accounts from their limited point of view, with the whole of our moral life hovering in the background.

There is a rich philosophical literature devoted to illuminating the language of moral discourse. The term *ought* has a particular fascination when it operates to sanction the doing of something that is morally worthy. Then there is *right* and *good* when they express approval of a moral sort; and many more projects that seek to enlighten us about the moral commitments we make when we express ourselves in particular ways.

Next, there are the champions of the brain. They seek to enlighten us about our moral life by explaining morally significant behavior in terms of brain activity. It adds to our understanding of what goes on in our brain, but what it adds to our understanding of ourselves is not at all obvious. All the activities of our life, including things that are of moral importance, have a subtlety and complexity that our mind, rather than our brain, comprehends. It is our mind, not our brain, that makes it possible for us to appreciate great literature as well as indulge ourselves in the pleasures of trash; *and it is our mind that provides the discriminations at the heart of our moral life.*

It is of course true that everything that goes on in human life requires a human brain; and that just how the brain makes possible whatever goes on in our mind, starting with consciousness itself, is perhaps the greatest of all mysteries. Still, there are those studying the operations of the brain who assume they can explain our moral life's subtleties and complexities in terms of the brain's activities. In any case, their study of the brain's operation takes place with only a limited awareness of what it is that constitutes the moral life for which a brain is necessary. A brain is necessary, but not sufficient, for us to carry on a moral life. But our mind is not only necessary. It is sufficient to provide everything we wish to

INTRODUCTION

know about our moral life as well as everything we need to carry on the mental activities that are at the heart of our moral life.

Evolutionary biology is another scientific discipline that has ventured to explain our moral life to us. Such Darwinian catchphrases as "survival of the fittest" are commonly misinterpreted and encourage a notion that it is an exercise of superior strength in the struggle to survive that is favored by nature. Evolutionary biology in the hands of enlightened scientists has a more morally hopeful message for us. There is much to be said for cooperation as a means of survival. It is true that there is much in nature to suggest that selfish behavior is beneficial and that altruism is an exceptional phenomenon. But a more hopeful message from science gives support to a morally reassuring view of the competition between our self-interest and our concern about others. It is just a fragment of our moral life, but an important one. The values of our moral life are independent of the facts of our natural life, but it is good to know that these facts do not present a challenge.

Philosophers have devoted a good deal of thought to the question of right conduct. How shall we judge what has been done, and how shall we decide what is the right thing to be done? There are two main camps: those who think there are some pre-existing moral principles that provide the answer; and those who think that the answer lies in an assessment of the consequences of what we do. There is a tendency to seek out helpful formulae, perhaps most notably those of the utilitarians, and those of the Kantians. While answering the questions is in principle an important part of our moral life, in practice we go about satisfying our craving for moral certainty in ways that dispense with theory-grounded formulae in favor of an intuitive sense of what's right that is tested critically when it comes up against opposing views.

Something called *morality* casts a long shadow over our lives. We have an innate susceptibility to being told what is right and what is wrong, and this is exploited by various sources of moral authority. Religion is perhaps the most prominent dispenser of morality, with its backing by an authority that cannot be challenged. But there are many lesser authorities that presume to tell us what we can and cannot do, sometimes with perfectly good reasons, and sometimes for reasons that are appallingly bad. There is an unfortunate tendency to think of morality as the sum and substance of our moral life. This dreadful mistake is reason enough to make clear our moral life's complexity.

Finally, there is the scientific study of a person's moral development, with particular emphasis on the moral development of children. The work of Jean Piaget and of Lawrence Kohlberg is particularly important in bringing to light that such things as a sense of fairness and responsibility, of right and wrong, and of compassion and empathy are all developed in childhood, just as all cognitive and intellectual capacities are. Seeing much of our internal moral life as dependent on a childhood development process is an important insight. But not surprisingly, the demands of our adult moral life require more sophisticated versions of these childhood moral assets.

An appreciation of our moral life is something important to all of us. We are all participants, and the more we know about it, the better we are able to enjoy its benefits and avoid its pitfalls.

* * *

It is the mainstays of our moral life that I consider in this book.

First, there is the question of exactly what it is that occupies us as we live our moral life. Being good, doing the right thing, these are the answers that come to mind. I have a different answer. Our moral life consists of *passing, and implementing, moral judgment concerning conduct*. Of course, it is conduct that really concerns us. But it is our judgments and the effect we give them that occupies us morally. Doing the right thing matters more than getting our judgment of it right. But as moral agents it is our coming to the right conclusion about what we do that is most important. It is meant to influence what we do and what consequences should follow. Our conduct has its significance as a moral event only by virtue of correct moral judgment. Conduct itself is morally inert.

It is conduct that is being judged. But what exactly is conduct? Our intuition gives us an answer, but looking more closely, the answer seems unreliable. There is the life of the mind with its own range of activities, and there are many in society – political and religious begin a list – who consider beliefs a form of conduct. And then there are questions about when activities that are not entirely in our control are still our conduct; and when events over which we exercise no influence at all are still to be accounted as our conduct because of some extraneous association we have with them

But then we come to the most pressing questions. What should be the basis of our moral judgments? We talk about morality, and we talk about moral sensibility. Understanding what we are talking about, and especially how important the difference between them is, is perhaps the most important, as well as the most neglected, part of our understanding of our moral life.

At the heart of our moral life are our relations with others. Each of us is a world in its own right, with individual personal interests that deserve the greatest respect. We live in a social setting, and this requires each of us to be concerned about the interests of others, each of whom is, like us, a world in its own right. The greatest moral challenges arise as we seek to make the accommodations required by our concern.

Historically, religion dominates our moral life, and a critical examination of its proper position is urgent business.

Another institution that is of great importance morally is the law. The fact that the law is the greatest achievement of our moral life is a generally neglected truth that needs to be made clear.

And finally, there is moral mischief. Abuse of our moral resources is a constant temptation, and I consider four examples that are chosen from among many interesting possibilities.

So much for the menu. Now for the meal!

1

WHAT IS OUR MORAL LIFE?

If we were deprived of our moral life we would be deprived of our humanity. Human beings we still would be, and still possessed of an extraordinary intelligence that sets us apart from all other creatures, but sadly unable to care about one another as we care about ourselves. The moral ingredient in our life keeps us from allowing our own interests to take precedence when the interests of others have a more pressing claim on us. Our intelligence can certainly compete in importance with our moral life, but it is our moral consciousness that makes us distinctively human. The awesome powers of artificial intelligence lack humanity because they lack the rudiments of a moral consciousness. Nothing speaks more eloquently of the importance of the missing ingredient.

One would suppose that a thing of such great importance could be easily described, that our moral life would stand out quite distinctly from the many other things that are its companions in the grand panorama of human consciousness. But that is not the case. In fact, the very term 'moral' seems plagued by a chronic vagueness. It is used in an offhand way to indicate approval, a declaration of attitude toward whatever it refers to. Ask exactly what it means and the response is likely to be something about right and wrong. The same judgment can be made about moves in a game of chess, or the way a passage in a Mozart sonata is played. Innumerable things we do may be thought to be right or wrong without any suggestion of a moral judgment being passed; and in all those cases we know how to explain what we mean. Morally right or wrong is different. We feel confident enough in rendering such a judgment, but we find it difficult to put our finger on just what it is that we are saying.

* * *

I suggest that when we claim something to be morally right or morally wrong we are passing a judgment that is grounded, explicitly or implicitly, in one or more of the elements of our moral consciousness. I will discuss more fully what these elements are in the next chapter, but I provide a preliminary account here. I suggest there are five sources of moral awareness that make up the content of our moral consciousness.

First, there are our ***Moral Sensibilities***. Without them we would be unable *to appreciate* sufficiently the concerns of others, and so unable to make the accommodations that are necessary for living together in a human society. Important though somewhat less pressing, without our Moral Sensibilities our ability to concern ourselves about the welfare of other living creatures would be greatly diminished.

Then there is ***Morality***. Our moral sensibilities are a personal resource that, like all our sensibilities, resides within us. Morality, however, has a source outside us, and rather than being something we experience, it is something that impresses itself on us as an exercise of authority. It relies on an ability to exploit our vulnerabilities, our feelings of guilt and shame, as well as our fear of the consequences of non-conformity or non-compliance.

A third element of moral consciousness is ***Being Responsible.*** *Our moral life consists in making moral judgments about conduct.* There are occurrences that concern us because they are in some way or other untoward; and other occurrences that are notable because they please us. In either case we are more often than not disposed to attribute the occurrence to some human agency, and then go on to blame or to praise whomever we deem to be responsible. But events do not always make clear exactly what their origins are, and conduct can be similarly reticent when it comes to making clear what, if any, its connections are to events that might be attributed to it. What's more, all activity is not conduct, and just what activity qualifies as conduct is itself an important question that affects being responsible. Our moral life is concerned to hold people answerable for their conduct, but only when they should be, and only to a degree warranted by how they are involved in the events that are of concern.

A fourth element is **Basic Personal Rights**. We are all entitled absolutely to have certain things about us respected by others for no better reason than that we are a person. We have the ability to compromise many entitlements we have, but there are also inalienable rights that we cannot give away. They belong to us more securely even than our blood or our kidneys. Some of these rights relate to our welfare, and some relate to our freedom. All of them shelter securely in the precincts of our moral life.

Finally, there is **Conscience**. It is anchored in our moral sensibilities, but it is more than simply an intuition alerting us to a moral concern in the offing. Conscience has three jobs. One is to stand in the way of any *temptation* to override the alarm our moral sensibilities have sounded. We have selfish interests that prompt us to do things our sensibilities do not find acceptable, and our conscience exercises restraint. The second job is after the fact, when our conscience bothers us about what we have done. Guilt plays a major role and makes Conscience a more effective actor in both jobs. The discomforts of Conscience can act as a deterrent, or they can prompt us to make amends for what we have done. And a third job is to ensure that our moral judgments are respected. This is especially important when the judgment is the outcome of moral controversy and represents what we should do on a particular occasion, regardless of the plausible case that was made on the other side.

* * *

These are the resources we have at our disposal in carrying on the activities of our moral life. But what exactly are those activities? *Passing moral judgment on conduct* is the answer. This may seem surprising. Is not how we conduct ourselves, rather than passing judgments, really what our moral life is all about? True enough, it is what we do that really concerns us. But becoming concerned means making judgments. What we do *needs to be considered* to be a matter of concern, and the sort of consideration that is appropriate is judgmental. It is what we conclude about what we do that is the substance of our moral life. Those conclusions are sometimes reached in the blink of an eye, at other times only after painful deliberation. They can be expressed prescriptively as moral maxims; they can be general propositions covering many items of conduct; or they can just be pronouncements on particular items of conduct.

The conduct being judged can take place at any time. If it took place in the past it may belong to history, or it may be something in the news that took place yesterday. It may be something that is going on now, or something suggested for the future – a serious proposal, or a fanciful conjecture.

And anyone's conduct is amenable to being judged morally. No one can escape judgment for whatever emerges from the mists of time. It is not only individual conduct that is susceptible to moral judgment, but the conduct of any group of individuals with a collective identity.

* * *

There are three sorts of moral judgments.

There are the standing judgments that we think of as *moral maxims*. A favorite of mine is in the Mishnah attributed to Hillel: "If I am not for me who is for me? And if I am just for me what am I? And if not now, then when?" And of course, there is "Love thy neighbor..." and "Do unto others...", as well as the many others that are iconic pronouncements standing above all moral controversy. They are *moral truths* that are never questioned, too remote to serve as a practical guide in everyday affairs, but still moral lodestars that remind us about our immutable relation to others.

The second sort of moral judgment is best thought of as *a principle*. These judgments take many different forms and are found in great abundance in the law. Unlike the moral maxims, these judgments are of practical importance. Some of them, like the moral maxims, are standing judgments ("No one shall profit from his own wrongdoing"). They are the sort of bedrock principles that serve as guides when the law is exercising the discretion allowed in its equitable jurisdiction. Much more numerous are the principles that resonate morally, in statutes and constitutions, treaties, and judicial opinions. Outside the law, there is an abundance of principles of the same sort that presume to tell us what is right or wrong as a moral matter.

Finally, there are the innumerable *ad hoc judgments* that are the outcome of morally significant controversies. Typically, such controversies take the form of attempted justifications in the face of what appears *prima facie* to be morally objectionable conduct. Our moral resources are martialed in support of one side or the other in a case of moral controversy, with the more persuasive argument entitling its proponent to a judgment resting on that argument. Such judgments may settle only one controversy, but they can become standing judgments with persuasive force for use in resolving future controversies of the same sort. In the law, their persuasive force can even be elevated and can enjoy the force of authority.

* * *

Moral judgment is judgment about conduct. But conduct is itself a slippery notion that I will try to pin down in the next chapter. There are two things that we must not do. We must not allow our moral judgments to range beyond conduct. We may conclude things about a person from the things he does, but it is only his conduct that can be the basis of our judgment. History, as well as the contemporary world, is replete with inquisitions and witch hunts that make the person, rather than his conduct, the target. And for the same reason, we must be careful in deciding what counts as conduct. We are entitled to enjoy a realm of personal privacy in which we are free of any moral intrusion, unjudged in what we think or say.

* * *

Moral judgments about conduct are not rendered just for their own sake. They are meant to influence our conduct, acting through constraints of conscience to keep us from doing what is wrong and encouraging us to do what we ought to do. Moral judgments do not, however, always influence conduct. They have another job. They make critical assessment of conduct possible, with consequences that are an important part of our moral life. We condemn, and sometimes we punish. Moral judgments serve to make us answerable for our conduct. What measures are taken in an attempt to set things right is itself a matter of great moral concern that requires consideration of principles of justice.

2

MORAL CONSCIOUSNESS

Consciousness can be thought of in two ways. There is consciousness itself, the mind awake and self-aware but not bound to be aware of anything else in particular. It is consciousness in the abstract, conceived as an empty vessel, available and waiting to be provided with content. Then there is consciousness as a panoply of things that we are aware of, the content of our consciousness whose collective experience is how we come to have a notion of consciousness in the first place.

Our consciousness is not passive, simply serving like a security camera to make us aware of things. Consciousness is intimately connected with the rest of our mental life, as well as our physical life, triggering emotions and ideas and actions in profusion. Our moral life's very existence depends on the awareness and its promptings that our moral consciousness provides.

There are five elements of moral consciousness to consider, and they are members of a joint moral enterprise. Our relations with others are their common concern, and more particularly, the concerns we have when our interests come into conflict with the interests of others; as well as the concerns that arise from our dependence on one another.

* * *

Moral Sensibility

Our sensibilities give us the ability to appreciate what we are conscious of. They give an initial meaning and importance to what we experience. Without our sensibilities, we would be deprived of the enjoyment that fine food affords us, of the pleasure that art gives us, of what is most enjoyable in our relations with others, as well as much of the satisfaction that our work and the work of others afford us. It is our powers of appreciation that allow us to make our life the happy experience it can be.

But our sensibilities also allow an appreciation of what is dreadful. They are responsible for an appreciation of the beauty in Turner's seascapes, but they are equally responsible for an appreciation of the horrors of the Holocaust.

The importance of appreciation is itself sadly underappreciated. What we experience needs our contribution – our appreciation of it – to give that experience the value it has for us, and that contribution is made by our sensibilities. They give us a personally enhanced experience.

In general, one's sensibilities are uniquely one's own, and this is especially clear when it comes to matters of taste. Still, there is amongst us a vast expanse of common ground, and this is especially clear when it comes to Moral Sensibility. We share a great deal in our appreciation of honesty, truthfulness, kindness, fairness, and love; of cruelty, suffering, injustice, deprivation; and of much, much more.

Our sensibility-enriched moral experiences are a combination of feelings and thoughts, and the experiences are for the most part negative. An experience of injustice or dishonesty asserts itself urgently and with a vivacity not normally found in an experience of justice or honesty. Our moral sensibilities are more excited by mischief than by worthiness.

Unhappily, we may act in ways that are a departure from the norm, ways that our Moral Sensibilities must deem perverse. And there are even psychopathic personalities whose Moral Sensibilities, like their eyesight, can fail them altogether, leaving them morally blind. Our Moral Sensibilities, moreover, do not provide the latitude of appreciation allowed us by our other sensibilities. Our aesthetic sensibilities give us free rein in choosing what we like and dislike in the art world, but there is a tighter rein when deciding about morally right and morally wrong.

And there are other differences. Most of those other things whose appreciation is an important part of our life are matters of self-satisfaction, and in that sense most of our other sensibilities are self-indulgent. Moral Sensibility is different. It is true that it provides us with the satisfactions that come from caring about others. But beyond that, it requires something of us. There is first a concern about the well-being of others. But, simply appreciating the suffering that another person is experiencing is not enough. One feels one must do whatever one can to make a difference. There is also concern about what one must not do. Appreciating how one might wrong another person comes with a warning sign that forbids doing it.

It is sometimes suggested that our Moral Sensibilities are in essence an identification through feeling. Empathy with those who suffer distress is thought to be an important virtue. Standing in another's shoes, or even better, in another's skin, is certainly to be recommended to overcome hard-heartedness, though the circumspection of a more arms-length appreciation is generally more helpful in devising effective remedies. And empathy comes with its own baggage. What prompts an empathetic engagement – what's behind such a strong identification in feeling – can often introduce irrelevant considerations that distort one's appreciation of the situation.

Concerning ourselves about others because we love them is an intensive form of appreciation. It puts our feelings center-stage, with whatever matters of concern those we love are experiencing made to play a supporting role in the drama. Love is a morally blessed self-indulgence, and it is a no less worthy feature of our moral life for providing an especially deep satisfaction for those who act out of love. Still, love must not be unbounded. Those we love must have their autonomy respected. Moral Sensibility itself requires nothing less.

Morality

The term "Morality" has negative overtones. There is a suggestion of something repressive and bullying in the air. It might well be needed, like police and prisons, but its existence is not a cause for rejoicing. And while

Morality is viewed as something respectable, like respectability itself it is often invoked to create an impression of upstandingness while a smell of hypocrisy and even duplicity surrounds it. Whatever is of genuine moral value will shy away from Morality. Simple caring and concern for others is not a high priority for Morality in the institutional forms in which it likes to present itself. Morality on its high horse is more likely than not to treat with disdain those immediate personal feelings we have for one another that need no outside support. Morality has a particular interest in bringing to heel whatever is a spontaneous product of a free spirit. It starts from the assumption that a person's inner workings are naturally primed for mischief and that Morality exists to thwart whatever escapades might be suggested by those malign endowments of our natural selves.

Morality is a creature of authority. Unlike Moral Sensibility, whose claims on us come from within us, Morality imposes itself from without but uses resources we provide to persuade us to submit to its dictates.

First, there is *guilt*. Feeling guilty is a universal and enduring part of human experience. It has its well-known origins in family life, where senior members are authority figures who exercise their authority over junior members, with prohibitions playing a prominent part in this exercise of authority. Disobedience or defiance, no matter how successful, will typically produce feelings of guilt, and those familiar feelings then become available for exploitation by other authorities who operate in a larger social context. Morality is a beneficiary of this process. Sexual morality, with its many and various taboos, has guilt as its mainstay, and this extends to sexual practices as well as the forbidden pleasures of the imagination. Religious morality is a wholesale purveyor of guilt, with the innumerable sins that are religion's stock-in-trade depending on guilt to give sin its vitality.

Then there is *shame*, another ready resource that Morality makes use of. All of us cherish our self-respect but find that it is not as robust as we might like it to be. When we are made to feel that we have done something wrong we become concerned about how others think of us. Shame is the wound that self-respect suffers when what others might think about one's transgression becomes a matter of concern. Morality can use the prospect of injury to self-respect as a threat. How we are thought of by others is a far greater concern than we like to admit, and the shame it produces is keenly felt. What we think others think of us affects what we think and feel about ourselves.

Next, there is *fear*. Religion makes notorious use of fear to ensure conformity to its doctrinal version of Morality. There is the hereafter to worry about, but also more immediate concern about one's fate here and now, where the higher power that religion represents can choose either to shine its light on us or cause us to suffer an unhappy fate, depending on whether or not we do what its Morality requires of us.

An even greater fear is the fear of social exclusion. Morality is now mainly a secular affair, and public opinion is now Morality in disguise. Though public opinion is diverse, and there is no single body of public opinion that represents *the one* Morality prevailing at any given time, there is a powerful constraint to identify with one strand or another. Morality serves as a powerful social force that binds people together, and finding oneself a disaffected outsider can be an uncomfortable experience.

But Morality's greatest strength is derived from a *need for the certainty that morality provides*. There is a pervasive belief in every human society that there is some sort of transcendent code defining what is right and what is wrong. The need for such a code precedes any particular idea of what form such a code might take, and ways in which that need is satisfied can take strange forms indeed. Nothing in the western world can compete in reverential importance with the Ten Commandments as a statement of Morality. Yet reading what is written there must surely leave one wondering why this is so. I suggest that whatever the historical accident that brought this about, the Ten Commandments serve to satisfy the abiding need for an unshakeable moral icon. Additionally, what is referred to as Judeo-Christian morality is an icon without an embodiment or even certifiable content. Its existence serves, nevertheless, to reassure us that there is after all a moral authority that preserves us from moral anarchy.

In addition to the enforcement resources we put at Morality's disposal, it has an important mechanism of its own that is most prominent when it appears in the form of close-minded ideology. From the everyday strictures of political correctness to the banishment of forbidden views on sensitive subjects there is *stigmatization* to deter deviation from the prevailing orthodoxies. It is Morality acting as a censor, protecting us from the speech or the writings of those deemed ideologically unfit and so offenders against right thinking. Those who bear such ideological stigmata are marked as pariahs and ineligible to enter any contest of ideas. It is Morality's most brazen pronouncement.

Stigmatization deserves a further word. It is carried on by fixing labels to whatever is to be stigmatized. It is Morality's smear tactic, and its success depends on the accusation remaining immune to any fact-finding investigation. Take *racism* as an example. In its current cavalier usage, who can say exactly when racism is or is not present? How different this is from *racial discrimination, racial prejudice, racial bigotry, racial hatred,* or *racial violence.* All of these can be determined to exist by pointing to evidence of an appropriate sort. Seeking evidence of racism is embarking on a fool's errand. An imputation of racism is stigmatization and is simply an invitation to regard what is stigmatized with opprobrium. Questioning whether there are facts to make such an invitation appropriate is asking an irrelevant question, much like asking if calling someone "a bastard" has a factual basis. Stigmatization is respectable name-calling, and its fact-exempt privileges make stigmatization a favorite of Morality.

Morality is a gun for hire, and not every morality can pass muster conducted by our Moral Sensibilities. One might think that Nazi morality is a morality in name only. It certainly must be deemed an abomination when judged by the Moral Sensibilities that ordinary Germans still had at the heart of their moral life. Still, however perverted, it was morally authoritative and purported to dictate how Germans should deal with other people in the light of Nazi assumptions about other people, as well as about how Germans should think of themselves. In that way, it qualified as a morality, albeit anathema to Moral Sensibility and Conscience.

Being Responsible

Our moral life consists of moral judgments about *conduct*. It is our way of holding ourselves morally responsible for what we do. This means it is important that we understand exactly what conduct is, what it is not, and why it is right to limit moral judgment to conduct.

Conduct is not the same thing as behavior. Animals and infants exhibit behavior of many different kinds, but they are not capable of engaging in conduct. Mobs of people, as well as people suffering serious mental abnormality, sometimes are just behaving and sometimes are engaging in conduct. It depends on whether they are deemed to be capable at the time of *choosing* to do, or not do, what they do. Being *capable of choosing to do, or not do,* is the key to being capable of conduct. And if inability to choose is a result of something one chose to do that deprived one of the ability, as far as moral judgment goes that may well leave such a person in the same position as someone who had the ability to choose.

The reason we think conduct, and not mere behavior, is needed for moral judgment is that *it isn't fair* to require someone who couldn't choose to do otherwise to be answerable for not doing otherwise.

Not all conduct consists of activity. Things one must do which are left undone can constitute negligent conduct, though no activity has taken place. Negligent conduct that does not consist of any activity can take place when one fails to exercise appropriate care in what one is doing. There is activity going on – I am driving – but I fail to turn on my headlights, which is negligent conduct, though not an activity. Moreover, conduct can be entirely passive. Simply being in possession of something can be conduct even though no associated activity is taking place. Could one have *chosen* not to be in possession, that is the crucial question upon which the existence of conduct depends. If one could not reasonably choose to avoid being in possession, *it would be unfair* to say that there was conduct to be judged. A test of fairness is ultimately decisive.

Conduct's exclusive domain is challenged by the contents of our mind. Why shouldn't what we think or believe also be subject to moral investigation and judgment?

As far as our thoughts go, unless we choose to disclose what we think our thoughts are unavailable for scrutiny by others. But what about when we ourselves are passing judgment on our thoughts? There are those who may encourage us to keep our minds pure. Religions, especially, are enthusiastic advocates, and there are also people who without any prompting are remorseless critics of the unkind thoughts they have. And then, of course, we sometimes do choose to share our thoughts with others. Are we inviting a moral judgment to be passed on what we think?

Our mental life has a randomness and spontaneity that makes it impossible for us to choose what passes through our mind. We lack the sort of control that is necessary if we are to be answerable for the thoughts we have. Even when we gather our thoughts and make guarded disclosures to others our thoughts enjoy an exemption from judgment just because they are *merely* thoughts and not something to which we are more committed. Moral judgment of our thoughts is therefore a folly, whether we undertake it ourselves or others presume to render such judgment. Not recognizing this, we can be unfair to ourselves by indulging our own morbid tendencies, or we can expose ourselves to the judgment of others who may have their own questionable motives for wanting to judge what we think.

Beliefs present a different challenge. Why should we not be morally accountable for our beliefs? Unlike our thoughts, our beliefs are affirmations that we are willing to defend with whatever degree of conviction seems appropriate. Expressing what we believe puts our beliefs on display and makes them subject to criticism. When we choose to express it, our belief has passed into the realm of conduct. Moral criticism of what we believe is not only unobjectionable, but a paradigm occasion for our moral life to assert itself. However, beliefs that remain unexpressed enjoy the same immunity from criticism as the rest of our undisclosed mental traffic. We may have settled beliefs and be committed to them, but not having chosen to express them we are entitled to have the innocence of our mind respected. Our mind has a right to privacy.

When we express ourselves what we have to say may be neither thoughts nor beliefs. We say things in order to make things happen, and we say things because we want to communicate to others what we have experienced. In general, when we choose to express ourselves, we are engaging in conduct and doing something that is amenable to moral criticism; and this applies both to what we have to say and to the saying of it. It is, in fact, our powers of expression that provide the most abundant examples of morally significant conduct.

Limiting moral judgment to what is done is of great importance. There is, however, a further challenge. There are religious or quasi-religious views of our moral life that speak of men's hearts and minds as the places where our moral life's most important activities are carried on, with what we do being simply outward manifestations of what is really important and takes place within us as part of our inner life.

There can hardly be a more insidious threat to our moral life than the shifting of concern from the generously fact-endowed world in which conduct takes place to the shadowy realm of our roaming thoughts, unbridled emotions, and figments of imagination, a place where facts are inconvenient obstacles to believing whatever one wishes to believe.

Another concern about conduct can emerge when we wish to distinguish between things that just happen and things that are done. We are always keen to discern human agency as the cause of untoward events. For one thing, it reassures us, no matter how unrealistically, that the terrible things that occur don't just happen by themselves but are in fact within our control; and that despite appearances we really are able to prevent them. As a bonus, we are provided with people whom we may blame and punish, "the responsible ones", thus gratifying our need to exact a measure of retributive justice.

In the interest of sound moral judgment, it is important to treat as causes of untoward events only those items of conduct that remain plausible candidates after there is a careful consideration of whether a person whose conduct it is could *reasonably* be expected to do otherwise than he did. If not, we must accept the fact that sometimes *things just happen*. Once again, considerations of fairness are ultimately decisive.

And then there is the matter of degrees of culpability. All conduct is not related to untoward events in the same way, and sound moral judgment must reflect that.

Conduct is sometimes dedicated to doing harm. At other times it is engaged in doing what is plainly harmful, but without any intention of causing harm. It is the difference between intending to do harm and intending to do only what, as a practical matter, makes harm unavoidable. Then there are other times when conduct is reckless, not itself the sort of thing that is more likely than not to cause harm, but nevertheless indifferent to the fact that it might well cause harm. And finally, there is conduct that is unobjectionable so long as it is carried on carefully, but in fact is being carried on without the care that avoids its dangers.

Once again it is what a person *has chosen to do* that determines his degree of culpability. There is a great deal of natural misadventure in the world, things that just happen; and some of it happens in the midst of what we happen to be doing. Morally sound judgment wants to take this into account so that only what a person has chosen do – his conduct – is taken into consideration in making a moral assessment. What is simply a matter of bad luck needs to be winnowed out so that we are answerable only for our conduct and not for what just happens to occur in its immediate vicinity at the same time. But if the occurrence of what is unintended is both notorious and foreseeable its occurrence is then not a matter of something "that just happened to occur".

Our conduct depends on our being able to choose to do otherwise. But when is it that we are not able to choose to do otherwise? There is a hornet's nest of difficulties here. Personal abnormalities deprive people of the ability to make a choice when they are overwhelmed by irresistible feelings, or when they cannot comprehend those things that one must be aware of in order to make a choice. Every bit as daunting are the compelling circumstances that can deprive a person of the ability to choose what to do – a gun at one's head, but a great deal more. Once again fairness is the test. Considering whatever constraints there may have been at the time, would it be fair to hold a person responsible for what he did? Sound moral judgments require an affirmative answer.

Rights

Rights are formidable. Possession of a right means one is free to do whatever that right entitles one to do. And in fact, we possess a right to do everything we normally do in living a trouble-free life. It is also true that we strive to keep our lives trouble-free by not doing what we have no right to do. Like M. Jourdain who didn't know he was speaking prose, we are unaware of the numberless rights we have. We take notice of a right only if the right is unusual, or our exercise of the right is challenged. Otherwise, our rights are silent companions that unobtrusively accompany us in everything we do.

But not all rights are passive creatures. Our most important rights are outspoken critics of what others can do to us, and they are constantly on the *qui vive* to protect us.

These rights are inherently ours as persons. They are inalienable possessions, as natural to us as our personality or our mentality, and no less enduring. *We have a right to our personal welfare. And we have a right to our personal freedom.* These two basic rights have no fixed limits and are best thought of as progenitors of the more concrete rights that take shape as part of our increasing moral maturity. There is recognition of these rights by political and legal institutions, but that is merely the conferring of an institutional backing that is needed to give our moral awakening the strength it needs to be an influence in society.

Basic welfare rights are protection against the harms we experience from violation of our physical integrity as well as from mental abuse. As persons we are entitled to live in an inviolable personal reserve that is not only a place of safety but a place where we can cultivate and enjoy those things that give us satisfaction. Rights of personal privacy, broadly conceived, are a moral imperative, as are rights that shield us from injury.

Basic rights concerned with freedom protect not only what we may do, but what we may say. But unlike welfare rights, the rights we have to do and to say what we like are in constant collision with the rights others have. Our autonomy is hedged in by the need to accommodate the rights of others. It is the business of government and other social authorities to seek morally acceptable compromise. Effective compromises can be achieved by measures of suppression, but a morally worthy compromise is one that both parties are bound to see is not unfair to either party.

Personal rights exist to protect us not only from other persons, but from the abuses that are a constant danger in the exercise of authority.

Life in society requires submission to many different kinds of authority – governmental, most notably, but others as well, including those inherent in family life, employment, social relations, education, and religion. Our personal rights allow us to live a life with others in which everything we value in ourselves as persons can survive and flourish.

Conscience

Conscience occupies an exalted place in our moral life. It is the forum of last resort in judging what appears to be morally tainted. Arguing against the dictates of conscience is futile, no matter how weighty or how alluring considerations on the other side might be. We may choose not to heed what conscience tells us is right, but we are then left with the burden of a troubled conscience that we cannot escape.

Conscience acts to deter us in anticipation of doing what is morally flawed. And it also plays a part after the fact when it encourages one to make amends as best one can. In both of these efforts, Conscience relies for its guidance on our Moral Sensibilities. Our Moral Sensibilities normally assert themselves when confronted with experiences that call for a moral appreciation. But our Conscience gives a voice to those sensibilities in the absence of the experience itself, when there is only a contemplation of such an experience, or when there are remorseful reminders of what has already taken place.

Acting as an agent of Moral Sensibility, Conscience brings to bear the guidance of Moral Sensibility. But what about Morality? Is our Conscience also carrying out orders from the hotchpotch of externally mandated edicts that comprise Morality? The answer is that Morality is served by our conscience only when Morality happens to be an advocate of what our sensibilities already tell us. Our Conscience is not available to act on behalf of whatever Morality declares to be wrong. Transgression of sexual taboos, unlike dishonest acts, are not the business of Conscience. Our Conscience is like our Moral Sensibilities. It cannot be traduced in its appreciation of what is right and what is wrong in order to make Morality's arbitrary demands a matter of Conscience.

Our conscience does enjoy a privileged existence, but it is not free of challenges to its exalted position.

Conscience is not immune to the blandishments of self-deception. We can convince ourselves that the mischief we do we can do with a clear Conscience. We can misconstrue the facts that count against what we are doing in a way that eases our Conscience. But our Conscience need not be a helpless victim of such deception and can insist on a version of the facts that will withstand scrutiny. It depends on the willingness of the person whose Conscience it is to act in good faith. The bad faith of a dishonest person can always devise a set of facts that will enlist the support of his Conscience, or at least keep it silent.

Then there is Conscience in overdrive. There are people for whom not putting a foot wrong is an obsession, and the scrupulous concern about not being in the wrong finds an especially welcoming home in such a person's moral life. A constantly troubling Conscience is more vexatious than a troubled Conscience. It seeks out reasons to feel guilty and ashamed in a world fraught with opportunities to do the wrong thing. A troubling Conscience is constantly asking, "Should I have done otherwise?". Mark Twain took note of this tendency when he said, "good friends, good books, and a sleepy conscience: that is the good life".

Conscience can be an altogether malign agent. George Bernard Shaw observed that there is nothing more dangerous than the conscience of a bigot; but that was before the Nazis came on the scene. Our Moral Sensibilities lend themselves to moral perversity in which hatred dominates a moral landscape and Conscience serves to justify killing what is hated. There is the example of the Nazi *Einsatzgruppen* who could engage in the hands-on slaughter of innocents with a clear Conscience. Members of the SS who said they were troubled by such duties were excused, but the majority carried out their orders with a remarkable insouciance as they imagined they were ridding the world of human rodents.

Religion is not a champion of Conscience. An inner voice is much more persuasive than the distant words from a higher realm that religion provides. The experience of our Conscience is a personal experience that speaks directly to us and is bound to be more compelling than the messages delivered by intermediaries who claim to be representatives of a remote higher power. And so, religion seeks to circumvent, or subvert, Conscience as a source of moral guidance, and instead offers comfort to the troubled Conscience through rituals of absolution and pastoral reassurance.

But there is worse. Religion makes use of Conscience as a weapon in religious warfare. In the clash of religious doctrines, it becomes a matter of Conscience to deny the truths of other Faiths, and even to seek the conversion of others to one's own Faith. Such open warfare has disappeared in the Western World, though in the East it still is in fashion, with religious antagonism a matter of Conscience, profound moral conviction, and garden variety bigotry.

* * *

Our moral life is a critical business. Passing judgment on conduct is the business of our moral life, and these are the resources that make such judgments distinctively moral.

But what about the enforcement of such judgments? Leaving the conduct judged hanging in the air is a disappointment. This is true; but the judgment stands as a guide for those who wish to know what is right and what is wrong. The same sensibilities that operated in reaching the judgment must do their best now to ensure it has an appropriate fate. Asking more is asking the impossible.

3

OURSELVES AND OTHERS

Our relations with others are the foundation of our moral life. More particularly, the concerns we have when our interests come into conflict with the interests of others; as well as the concerns that arise from our dependence on one another. As moral creatures we are not self-obsessed monsters, making our way through life with any concern for others making an appearance only when strictly required. We are compelled to recognize the simple truth that others are as important as we are and that their self-interest is as urgent a matter as our own.

But this simple truth is challenged by a countervailing idea. Our own basic interests must be attended to first, since if we do not give them priority our own existence can come to an end summarily, and with it our ability to help others. Indeed, as a general preposition preventing our own existence from coming to an end or even just avoiding a serious personal loss are sufficiently important in themselves to justify doing whatever is needed to make sure that such a disaster does not happen. For while we recognize that other lives are no less important than our own, we are nevertheless on solid ground in acting as though our own lives are of greater importance when our lives are threatened in some fundamental way. And consider this. Ideally, others with a greater need have at least as good a claim as I do to all the money I have that I don't need. But does such a moral truth carry the day when self-interest is allowed to make its case in the full context of our life? The question then becomes "Just how important is our moral life? Must it always prevail whenever it asserts itself?"

Our lives do seem to have a stubborn integrity that resists extreme subordination to the interests of others no matter how strong their moral case might be. We are always entitled to resist what amounts to moral self-abuse. We may admire those who practice it, but that does not mean we ought to follow their example.

Nature has endowed us with a spare kidney. There are others whose lives depend on a transplant from a donor. Are we in any way morally deficient in not volunteering the kidney we do not need? The right moral judgment requires a measure of moral sophistication. Moral considerations must be weighed against other sorts of considerations that make taking a kidney a formidable intrusion into the tranquility of one's life and so to be avoided unless necessary. Those who volunteer their kidneys have unquestionably done something of extraordinary moral worth. But others of us who fail to follow suit are not morally deficient. We have not been selfishly indifferent but have simply chosen to respect the balance between our interests and the interests of others that is inherent in the human situation. We have not become moral heroes, but neither have we compromised our moral integrity. We looked after ourselves as, morally, we are entitled to do.

It is a matter of *justification*, which is a familiar enough concept within mainstream moral practice. In extreme circumstances, one is entitled to kill to protect oneself, though taking another's life is morally wrong. Similarly, when moral demands on us are extreme, we are entitled to demur on the grounds that a requirement to help others does not apply when the consequences to oneself are unacceptably onerous. Unless our lives are a moral shambles to begin with, being morally decent does not require us to turn our lives upside down. Furthermore, the person who donates his kidney is not because of that a person of greater moral attainment. Our moral life is not a competitive enterprise in which those who do something of extraordinary moral worth are to be accounted morally superior people. Moral heroics call for applause, but judging the moral worth of a person calls for a judgment of how his life is lived through time.

There are less extreme cases that are more challenging. Nature has endowed us with more blood than we need. At the same time, there are shortages of much-needed blood in blood banks. Do we have a moral duty to give some of the blood we don't need to help fill the need at the blood bank? Are we remiss if we fail to contribute? This seems to be an intermediate case. We are not moral heroes if we make a contribution, but neither are we failing in a moral duty if we ignore the call for blood donors, at least when the circumstances are not truly exceptional. It seems that when the consequences of inaction are less than alarming, inaction may be justified. We have failed to do something that is morally creditable, yet at the same time have not acted discreditably.

But in fact, there is no need for any justification. We need no special circumstances to let us off the hook. We have simply chosen to travel on a broad boulevard of moral neutrality. A world without such morally free zones would be a world in which freedom as we know it would not exist, a world in which we are constantly harassed and called to account by a persistent inner judgmentalism. In the law, there is the idea that certain matters are *simply not justiciable*. In our moral life, we must respect a corresponding idea. A great deal in our life is *simply not moralizeable*.

* * *

I want now to consider how as morally sensitive creatures we might reconcile the two competing claims that are made on us as we struggle to live a satisfying life of our own, while still helping others when they need our help. Sometimes helping others is a matter of duty, rather than choice, and the question is when one is justified in ignoring one's duty. When it is a matter of choice, how is one to decide whether one's own interests or those of others are of paramount moral importance, or indeed whether moral importance is even the ultimate question?

These are not simply the dilemmas encountered by moral theorists thinking through abstract moral concerns. We are confronted throughout our lives with the competing claims of "me or you, us or them." Of course, what we want may be things that benefit others rather than ourselves, but even then it is a self-gratifying activity that has its place alongside those other activities in which we satisfy ourselves by doing what is good just for ourselves. It is self-satisfaction that prompts us to act in both sorts of cases.

Is it possible, then, to determine the moral worth of an act by the satisfaction it affords the actor? Are the satisfactions of the same sort when we benefit ourselves and when we benefit others? Is there a distinction to be observed here between *the different qualities* of satisfaction in one case and the other? If so, might the different quality of satisfaction be of crucial importance in determining a difference in moral worth?

* * *

It seems beyond dispute that the satisfaction produced by owning and driving a Rolls Royce is of a *morally inferior quality* to the satisfaction produced by helping a friend in distress. And this is so regardless of *the amount* of satisfaction in each case. Moral worth does not depend simply on how good the act makes the actor feel. Satisfactions are not all of the same sort, and those that are derived from helping others are of a superior quality to those that result from acts of wanton self-indulgence. One can easily test this by comparing one's experience of doing what benefits someone else with the experience of benefiting only oneself, with the scale of the benefit being comparable in the two cases.

There is something mysterious and intriguing about differences in the quality of satisfaction. We seem to be made in a way that produces in us deeper and more abiding satisfactions when the good we do is not self-interested. When we see someone else and not ourselves benefiting from what we do there is a dividend in self-esteem that is the ultimate reward. Still, it would not be quite right to say that we help others because the experience for us is of a superior sort. It is because of something deeper in us, with the greater pleasure it gives us an incidental consequence.

* * *

I want to suggest that the mystery of self-satisfaction through altruism and self-sacrifice can be better understood if we become clearer about the distinction between ourselves and others.

First of all, to what extent are we really separate beings? There can be no doubt that we each have our own private history, and that we draw on it to provide ourselves with a unique and distinctive identity. The events of my life mark me out as the person I am, and there is no possibility of anyone else suddenly showing up with exactly the same personal history. The most important consequence of this historical uniqueness is the uniqueness of our repertory of experiences. It is not just *the particular events* determining our repertory of experience that are unique. It is *our particular experiences of those events* that have no duplication.

Indeed, the same event may be experienced by us and by others, and what is then common in the different experiences of the event may be thought of as belonging to the event itself. But though there are common elements, each person's experience of the same event will be unique to the person experiencing it *because of the uniqueness of that person's history of experiences* and the unique effect on that person of such a unique history. In speaking of events in a person's history, I am of course including those internal events that by their nature must be private and not directly accessible by others, and which are of the greatest importance in guaranteeing the uniqueness of each personal identity. *It is our sensibilities at work, providing us with our own personal appreciation of what we experience.*

It is true, of course, that we have our separate bodies to reassure us that we are separate creatures. This physical separation is an immense convenience in allowing us to live our separate lives as autonomous creatures, but it is not what sustains us in the idea that we each have a distinct and unique identity. We do recognize physical differences in sufficient variety to ensure uniqueness to each person, but that has only a superficial bearing on identity. Think of identical twins that for practical purposes are so alike physically as to be indistinguishable. Yet they have separate identities that are unique, the same as everyone else.

* * *

The way we think of ourselves implicates both body and mind, and the same is true about the way we think of others. But we have direct access only to the physical self that we encounter in others, while having direct access to both our mind and our body. We are therefore naturally more involved in what goes on in our mind than we are in what goes on in the mind of others. Beyond what goes on in our mind, it is our very consciousness itself that provides us with an exclusive sense of ourself. This exclusive intimacy within ourselves creates a natural bias toward greater concern about ourselves than about others. Because of its immediacy we can be aware of what is going on in our own interior life in a way that's impossible regarding the inner workings of others, however great our concern about them might be. And what is going on is not a series of passive happenings. Living our lives is an activity that our mind not only experiences, but initiates and seeks to control.

The fact that this is true for each of us means that each of us is an island unto himself in the first instance, though that is not the end of the story. We do have ways of communicating ourselves to others, and we have a strong wish to do so. We may be separate and cannot offer others direct access to our inner selves, but we want nevertheless to avoid isolation. Even though what is going on within another person in a hidden realm is privileged information, there is a desire to share much of it, if only to avoid loneliness and seek reassurance.

We are responsive to such moments of openness in others because we ourselves want to escape the solitary confinement that is inherently the sad fate of the self. And so, we have a concern about others that is rooted in our own sense of isolation. There is also the more obvious fact that in so many ways we depend on others for our very survival, and because of that we recognize a reciprocal obligation to those who depend on us. But it is the need to escape the torments of loneliness that is the inherent condition of the self that drives us even more powerfully to seek a welcoming contact with others.

It is often thought that when we reach out to help others we are doing something that we are not really obliged to do and that such acts should therefore be regarded as morally supererogatory – not truly exceptional, yet more than is called for by the stark facts of the human condition.

This, I think, is a serious misconception. Because of the dependence of each of us on others, and because of the need to escape from the isolation of the self, when we help others we are doing what comes naturally as a matter of self-interest.

* * *

Ourselves and others: two separate but interdependent selves we certainly are. But being separate does not mean that we do not have a great deal in common. And our separate and distinct identities are not compromised by our efforts to break down the barriers that separate us. We are not threatened with a loss of our separate identity by sympathetic and empathetic engagement with others. Quite the contrary. We have an enlarged consciousness of ourselves, understanding ourselves better through an understanding of others that treats them as our vicarious selves. Taking others on board in that way tends to dispel the self-protective apprehensiveness that is naturally there when we relate to one another simply as strangers.

* * *

But, there is more than sympathy and empathy to this story. Others *become part of us* through the intimacy of acquaintance and dependence. There are those with whom we feel we have an especially close relationship and who are a fixed part of our lives. And we have them not only as part of our lives, but as part of ourselves. It is true that they are part of us only as long as they are a fixture in our life. And it is true that they remain a separate self even though they occupy a position of fixed intimacy in our lives. But even though they retain their separateness they are assimilated in our consciousness and our affective life in a way that makes them part of us. Though we remain separate, it becomes difficult, if not impossible, to discern the point at which our concern for them is not also a part of our concern for ourselves.

It is especially important to note how attachment to these people differs from our attachment to even the most familiar and best-loved objects in our lives. *Though taking care of ourselves is an existential priority, other people who are closest to us matter to us as much as we matter to ourselves. It is this that makes them seem a part of ourselves.* And so, we have here a further suggestion of why we care about others who are close to us. It is because they seem to be part of the interior world that we think of as ourself, something we care about because it seems a part of us.

* * *

There is a further point of importance that has a bearing on our conception of ourself. One of the darkest secrets of the self is its origins. We like to think that the person we are has been determined by the natural order of things. We have a sense of our existence being inevitable. Those who came before us in the ancestral parade that is our personal history were destined to play their part in bringing us into existence. But of course, this is nonsense. Just think of all of the crucially important chance meetings that were necessary, and of the many other things that were necessary that were sheer happenstance. Just think of the many decisions that could easily have been otherwise, with outcomes that would not have provided what was needed to bring us into being. These unwelcome truths undermine the notion we have of ourself as someone who was meant to be.

And alas, we must also dispel any lingering misconceptions about our immediate origins. There is a romantic notion that not only were our parents bound to meet and to mate, but that they were bound to provide the particular sperm and ovum whose happy meeting resulted in the particular person we are. Of course, we know better, but the belief lingers on because it helps us feel secure in our identity. We depend on those who are closest to us for an assurance that who we think we are has the certainty of historic inevitability. No wonder our concerns for them are an extension of concern for ourselves.

Our feelings of concern about others have their home in our relations with those who are close to us. But these feelings are not restricted to that intimate circle. There is not the same intensity of feelings toward others who are not part of our lives, but through the sympathetic and empathetic resources of our imagination, they become people who matter to us. Those close to us are part of our lives, and even without our becoming aware of it, those closest become part of how we define ourselves. But even without being part of our lives, much less part of us, others still do matter to us.

* * *

I have suggested some reasons why the separation between ourselves and others is not as great as we think. One might suppose this would promote a more welcoming attitude toward others, but in fact, we often find ourselves acting in opposition to others, making it clear that interdependence and the intimacy of kinship can be an inconvenience that must be overcome as we strive to assert our individuality. Making our mark as individuals can be at least as important to us as caring about one another. There are urgent questions that need to be answered.

How much of our limited resources should we be devoting to helping those who need our help? Money is the chief resource, but there is also time that can be diverted from what benefits us and directed instead to what benefits others.

When should we give way in a competition with others for what we both want? Helping others is one thing. Sacrificing what one wants for oneself to satisfy the needs of someone whose needs are greater than one's own is something else.

And then there is the underlying question of when we should bother to pay attention to moral considerations at all. Moral concerns are a guardian, keeping us from abusing others as we carry on legitimate activities. But they can interfere with what we are doing, demanding a moral fastidiousness that has us tiptoeing lest someone be hurt, or just offended, or even just moved to take a critical view of what we are doing. Intimidating moral concerns can keep us in bondage as we seek to live our lives in a reasonable way as free human beings.

* * *

To answer these questions, we must turn to our social life. I have been considering the great debt we owe to others for our sense of our self.

How we see ourselves depends to a considerable extent on how we see others with whom we choose to identify ourselves. But we are social creatures as well as individuals in our own right. There are groups to which we belong, and these groups also have distinctive identifying features. We are known to ourselves and to others not only by the unique and distinctive idiosyncratic features that mark us out as individuals, but also by the distinctive features of the groups to which we belong. Prominent among these features are the rules and customs that guide members of a group in their relations with one another.

Expectations of what is owed to one another are of paramount importance in the group. There are no ready formulae to be applied to answer the questions I have raised. There is no *morally* correct apportionment of resources to be made between oneself and others. But there are limits on selfishness that affects others. Such limits are necessary if the cooperation necessary for harmonious survival is to exist. It is *what one is not permitted to do and what one is not permitted to have* that serves as a moral guideline, with anything one is obligated to do simply serving in support of that. There are no simple rules of what to do that one can rely on to do the right thing, only *limits* on what one can do if morally unacceptable self-indulgence is to be avoided.

Even the simplest moral recommendations reflect this restrictive approach. Doing unto others as you would have them do to you tells you not to treat other people in a way that you would not like to be treated yourself. It is not telling you to think about what you would like to do to someone else, and then go ahead and do it so long as you would be willing to have the same thing done to you. Love thy neighbor as you love yourself tells you not to have less concern for others than you have for yourself. It is not telling you that you must share with others whatever satisfactions you manage to have in your own life.

There are celebrations of extreme, even ultimate, self-sacrifice in love and in war. Such stories are romantic denials of the self for the sake of others. But they are outside the realm of the moral world. They lack value as a moral exhortation since really, they are treating the person whose acts are celebrated as someone whose human dignity and well-being are no longer things of importance, a person whose moral standing is made irrelevant by what seems a more exalted cause that he has chosen and that has consumed him.

* * *

Helping others is a supreme moral virtue that has a less ambitious companion. It is *concern for others*. Contributions to charities and political support for policies that help those in need are less demanding than the sort of help that requires personal involvement in dealing with the troubles others have. But *concern for others* can take a different form, one that is not affirmative, but simply cautionary.

As we proceed to do things that suit us, we sometimes find ourselves doing what others might find harmful to them. There are dangerous acts that the criminal law seeks to protect against, both acts causing harm and acts that just threaten it. But much more common are those activities that might cause harm to others and can be counted on to excite moral concern, though they are free of criminal liability. Doing things in a way that is unfair even though not illegal is grounds for moral disapproval. Carelessness or thoughtlessness in carrying on perfectly legitimate activities are also susceptible to moral criticism, though no crime has been committed.

And so there emerges another dimension to our moral concerns. It is not simply a matter of helping others in need of help, or at least being concerned that their needs are being met. Our moral life also extends to doing those things that we do for ourselves in a way that takes proper account of the harm to others that might result from it. *Our life as caring creatures has two dimensions.* First, we seek to benefit others, most urgently when they are in need of our help, but also more generally when we are able to improve their lives for them. And then, as caring creatures, we carry on our own lives in a way that avoids harming others in a world that conspires to make that a constant challenge.

* * *

Avoiding doing harm exhibits a clear concern for the well-being of others, and it passes moral scrutiny with flying colors; while failure to concern oneself with the harm one causes, or is likely to cause, even though no harm is meant, is a moral deficiency. But what about conduct that is meant to do harm? The answer will seem obvious. What could be more morally wrong than conduct that has doing harm as its object? Take murder, for example. *Thou shalt not kill.* What plainer example of moral interdiction could there be? Yet things are not quite that simple.

I have been arguing that the moral is about concern for others, and especially when that concern calls for some sacrifice of things of importance to oneself. Killing someone does indeed suggest a lack of concern for the victim, but important as that is, it leaves a lot that is important unsaid. Saying murder is morally wrong is an underwhelming observation. Morally wrong indeed, but there is something about murder that makes mere moral criticism seem hopelessly inadequate. Something is missing, and what is missing is what is most important.

We depend on the goodwill of others for their moral bounty, but fortunately, we have something more reliable when it comes to not being harmed. We are not simply at the mercy of others, hoping that they will be morally disposed to forebear from hurting us. A world in which some are simply at the mercy of others, no matter how generous that mercy might be, would be a world in which life would be intolerably precarious. And so, we have protection against harm in the form of *basic personal rights*. The most serious crimes are a violation of such rights, at least those crimes that cause serious harm to a person. But it is not the criminal law that creates such rights. The rights are there to begin with, and we use the criminal law to give the rights the teeth we want them to have. These rights take precedence over the judgments of our moral life, just as self-preservation must take precedence over helping others. They are rights that serve as the basis of moral judgments, but they have an importance that transcends the merely moral.

In short, conduct that is meant to do serious personal harm does indeed constitute a lack of concern for the victim, and so is morally wrong. But much more important, it violates a *basic personal right* whose importance puts our moral life in the shade.

* * *

The paramount importance of our own basic personal rights is an assurance that each of us has against the aggression of others. We are not left to the moral mercies of others in a struggle to survive and to preserve the well-being we enjoy. Each of us has a moral life that imposes on us a duty of caring about others. But each of us also has rights that protect us from the extreme derelictions of others when those derelictions consist of doing us serious harm. For some people, it is their moral resources, and especially their conscience, that keep them from harming others, while for others it is the strictures of the law or the weight of social disapproval. But all of us, as possible victims of what others will do, do not live our lives depending simply on the restraint that others will exercise to preserve us from harm. As people in civilized society, we are all endowed with enforceable claims against others based on our inalienable rights. Without them, we should have to live as supplicants hoping to be able to appeal successfully to the moral instincts of others to do us no harm.

This is straightforward when others are out to harm us, but less so when others wish us no harm but simply find us standing in the way of what they want. Cases of pure malice are always there, where harming is just what the doctor ordered to even the score, or even just to satisfy some random malevolent appetite. But more often there is no malice. What we want is perfectly understandable, but alas, the means of getting it involves causing others to suffer some harm. In life, there is often a mismatch of things desired and the means available to obtain them while still respecting the well-being of others. And so, we all need a carapace of *basic personal rights* that protects us against the harms that life with others makes an eminently credible threat.

Basic personal rights are something we enjoy as certainly as our heartbeats or the air that fills our lungs. They are part of our moral life, but they are more than that. They are more than something that is owed to us as a matter of basic human decency. Nothing in my life is more important than my right to be free of the harms that take place when the most serious personal crimes are committed.

4

RELIGION AND OUR MORAL LIFE

Nothing lays claim to our moral life more confidently than religion. It prescribes rights and wrongs in a no-nonsense fashion that well suits a divine source. Sometimes proclamations come directly from the divinity, but more often there has been a delegation to those who purport to act on behalf of this higher power, with no shortage of disputes about whose word truly represents the divine message.

Religion is a strange proprietor of our moral life. Religion exists to satisfy deep human needs. There is first of all the fact of death to which we must somehow reconcile ourselves. Religion provides reassurance that the stark reality of personal annihilation is not the whole story, that there is a continued existence that makes the prospect of death a less dreadful business.

Then there is fate. We are all of us throughout our lives concerned to avoid misfortune. Everything we value in life – our personal well-being, our material well-being, being loved, and so much more – can be taken from us when things over which we have no control happen to us. But a divine power that looks after us can prevent such terrible things from happening. We may be powerless, but there is a higher power that is all-powerful. That higher power may even go the extra mile for us by inflicting misfortune on those who deserve it.

But what place does our moral life have in this story?

I suggest that it helps in the job of making death seem less awful. Having lived what religion deems a morally respectable life one may expect to be rewarded with an eternal existence. Religion offers hope in our natural life by promising a much-to-be-desired supernatural life after death to those whose life before death passes religion's moral assessment.

Moral rectitude plays a similar role in keeping us free of the dreaded things that can befall us in life. Quite simply, if we are good, we are not only spared misfortune but are blessed with good fortune; and if we are bad, we are visited with those things we wish to avoid. It is true that in many religions there are other things that are believed to influence fate, things such as rituals having magical properties as well as supplications through prayer that make use of flattery and praise in order to gain divine favor. Still, moral excellence seems like the most wholesome way to influence divine judgment, not least because it leaves responsibility for our fate in our own hands.

* * *

Religion also offers a court of last resort for unrequited injustices. The promise of divine justice makes human injustice seem less unfair. We are plagued throughout our lives by grievances, large and small. We have devised human institutions to set things right and prevent the anguish we will suffer if an injustice is allowed to persist. But human institutions are imperfect, and when they fail to do justice religion comes to the rescue. There is a higher realm in which a higher power can be appealed to. Even if it does not remedy the injustice, by providing a more generous moral setting religion can make the injustice seem less important, and so less painful.

* * *

Religion is an exploiter of our moral life, making use of it to reassure us regarding those concerns of ours that give religion its *raison d'etre*. The substance of the Morality that religion makes use of comes from our moral sensibilities, but religion, as an external authority, treats moral sensibilities as the bases of moral obligations. It is no longer a matter of what we must do in good conscience, but rather what we must do to be in conformity with religion's authority. This is not simply compliance with rules that we have a duty to abide by as members of a religious group. Rather, the obligation to conform is made compelling by a fear of the consequences of transgression. There are our feelings of guilt and shame that religion is always ready to exploit, but above all a fear of incurring divine displeasure.

Religion carries on its business in the region of the unknown where faith takes the place of experience, and where religion's authority is absolute. A more congenial place for Morality to flourish is hard to imagine. Any moral edict religion chooses to utter is shielded from the normal buffeting of moral controversy by its sacred origin. Religion's Morality has an advantage over our inner moral promptings. Being an *external authority* it is able to claim objectivity, and so a certain *prima facie* correctness in its pronouncements. And when it is religion that is the source of Morality's authority Morality enjoys the additional prestige that follows from its being sacred. No wonder religion is commonly regarded as the fountainhead of our moral life.

* * *

Organized religion espouses its Morality and puts it to work to deal with life's most anguishing concerns. But all religion is not organized and the individual state of mind that fosters religious experience can be fertile ground for the production of moral insights. What we owe to one another can be seen especially clearly when the spiritual state of mind that fosters religious experience is occupied by concerns about one's fellow man. The forces that drive a person to religion as a refuge from the harshness of ordinary life also make the altruistic messages of moral sensibility a welcome respite.

Alas, religion will not leave well enough alone. Alongside an empathetic concern for others, religion develops an obsessive interest in self-excoriation. Religion intensifies guilt and brings it to an elevated level of experience in the form of sin. When there is sin, whatever its cause may be, it is deemed an offense against God. Simple moral truths that we know as a matter of moral sensibility are appropriated by religious Morality and declared, for added emphasis, to be sin. In this way, religion expropriates personal moral experience and uses it to exercise dominion over its faithful flock. That, however, is not the whole story of sin. Religion has mechanisms of redemption. Sin can be expiated. There is confession and there is atonement to lift the burden of sin, as well as rituals to purge the stain of sinfulness. Sin's greatest importance is not its acting as a deterrent threat. It is more important as an opportunity for absolution and a release from the anguish of sinfulness.

But in addition to sin's encouraging feelings of hostility toward oneself, there is religion's hostility toward other religions. It is certainly true that we now live in a time when open hostility has abated, at least in Christian societies, where ecumenism has become a cause extending beyond the reconciliation of the various parts of the Christian religion. But though religious conflict is now a less prominent feature of history than in the past, organized religion is not an institution that promotes the positive messages of our moral life across religious boundaries. Each religion has its own relationship with a higher realm which it guards jealously, and this inevitably tends to promote an unsympathetic attitude toward other religions and their otherworldly claims. And it is the members of other religions who are treated with disdain. The demands for sympathetic understanding that moral sensibility makes on us are disregarded when one religion confronts another and there is an authoritative voice from on high that contradicts what our beleaguered conscience tells us is right. This should come as no surprise. When religion has something to say, conscience is expected to be silent.

* * *

Religion establishes an intimacy with the divine by endowing the divine with human characteristics. The Greek gods were portrayed shamelessly as humans writ large, living storied lives that incorporated the best and the worst of human life. And the God of the Hebrew Bible, while not living an adventurous life, still displays human emotions and interacts with human figures in much the same way that these figures interact with one another. God as a moral role model leaves a good deal to be desired. Anger, jealousy, and vindictiveness are prominent features, with self-regarding concerns dominating the divine personality. And it is not only in setting a questionable example that God has a morally chequered career in the Bible. Many laws that bear his imprimatur are morally flawed, at least when viewed in the light of well-established standards that prevail in modern times. Religion espouses moral precepts whose divine origin ensures their timelessness, and the very idea of our having a moral development, as we move from darkness into light, is not a notion that finds a welcoming place in most religions.

* * *

A word about theodicy.

Religion is constantly embarrassed by reality, and most particularly by the mismatch between the things people do and the way things turn out for them. No good deed goes unpunished is a light-hearted expression of this, while examples of good fortune in the carrying on of morally deplorable activities are legion. The part of religion that links our fate to our moral life must explain itself. It is, after all, one of religion's most important claims that doing what is right is rewarded by the higher power that determines our fate, while wrongdoing results in the opposite. And most troubling is the terrible things that happen to the innocent souls that have done nothing to deserve the misfortune that has befallen them. How can we justify God's ways in the face of such moral chaos? God's very existence can come into question when we consider the scale of cosmic injustice that prevails in the world.

Theodicy is the effort made to reconcile the idea of God as ensuring justice with the bitter truth of the way the world is; and this is not just an occasional concern, but a constantly recurring worry.

The obvious way to do this is by having God confer a measure of freedom on the human creatures who are the pride of his creation. But at what price? If God washes his hands of what we do he undermines our reason for believing in his existence. It is his power to deal with us according to how well we conform to his moral precepts that gives us a reason to believe in him. The evil in the world may make us skeptical, but we must find a way to bolster our faith that God remains in charge.

The most radical suggestion came from Ovadia Yosef, a Sephardic Chief Rabbi in Israel.

No event in human history surpasses the Holocaust as a challenge to belief in God. Ovadia Yosef suggested that the Jews who were victims of the Holocaust had somehow become the bearers of the souls of others who were being punished by God for their transgressions. What transgressions could possibly merit such punishment was left unanswered, as was why and how there had been such a transmigration of souls in the first place. God was being portrayed as having employed the SS to administer divine justice. A lunatic's fantasy, you might think, and what amounted to moral depravity in this grotesque attempt to justify the Holocaust and save God's good name.

Ovadia Yosef, however, remained a revered figure, with hundreds of thousands attending his funeral. In the abstract, perhaps this can be viewed as the end justifying the means. What, after all, could be a more important undertaking than bolstering faith in God when that faith is subject to its most severe testing, so severe that any means is justified?

* * *

I tell this as a cautionary tale. When human minds become possessed by the need to serve God our moral life can be in great danger. It is true that there are those who feel they are carrying on God's work when they devote their lives to helping others in ways that can only be admired as a flourishing of our moral life. But unfortunately, a concern with doing God's work can become an encouragement to do what is morally deplorable. And while good works require no religious support, the malign things that are done in God's name are always sheltered, if not encouraged, by religious belief.

* * *

It is clear that religion is a moral parasite. Our internal moral resources – our moral sensibilities – provide religion with what is worthwhile in religion; but religion has its own agenda that gives us little of moral worth in return. Even more shameful is religion's mischief that undermines our moral life.

5

LAW AND OUR MORAL LIFE

In our moral life we are very busy rendering moral judgments. We pass judgment on what we propose to do as well as what we are doing and what we have done. And our moral jurisdiction is vast. It extends beyond us to whatever there is in the world that can be judged morally. It is true that at times we do feel that things far removed from us in time or place are simply too alien and really beyond our moral competence. Yet if we choose to, we can employ our moral resources to subject everyone and everything throughout the world, past and present, to moral scrutiny. This is a truly awesome power.

Then there is the law. The law is the creation of a particular human community that it is designed to serve, and so its jurisdiction is far more limited, with the law itself determining the boundaries of its own jurisdiction. But though more limited in scope, the law has a considerable advantage.

Unlike our moral resources, the law speaks with a definite authority. Whatever it has to say has an origin that commands a general allegiance and respect. And there is another important difference. The law has teeth that ensure enforcement of whatever it has to say.

Our moral life, on the other hand, when it purports to have authority only has authority in a metaphorical sense. Orthodox religion, for example, must rely on the fanciful extravagance of its moral pronouncements having a divine origin; and for an enforcement mechanism there is only some imagined form of divine retribution. Furthermore, the law strives for, and generally achieves, great clarity in conveying what it wishes to tell us. Our moral life, while expressing itself forcefully enough, expresses itself without the specificity that the law insists on, and though littered with many stories and maxims that capture moral insight, our moral life mainly depends on *ad hoc* promptings that suit the occasion.

And yet it is the law that must answer to a moral reckoning, and not the other way round. One might have thought that the social consensus and political will that the law represents would make any moral objections to it an interesting curiosity, at best something for consideration if and when the political climate is more favorable, but at present out-of-step in a democratic society. Not so. Moral objections must be confronted here and now.

The main reason moral concerns about the law must take precedence is that the practical power the law possesses is a constant threat to our moral life. Law that is morally flawed is objectionable not only because of the harm done by its implementation but also because having it on the books taints our moral life. It confers on what is morally defective the awesome prestige of the law's authority.

* * *

Though sound moral criticism must prevail when it conflicts with what the law says, still the presumption remains that the law must be obeyed. Overcoming that presumption is an easy matter when the law serves a manifestly evil purpose, or even when it is simply controversial but unacceptable in good conscience within the bounds of good-faith controversy. Disobeying the Nuremberg Laws needs no justifications, but defying laws that require separate but equal facilities for members of different races is justified quite simply as a matter of good conscience.

The mistake is imagining that because something is the law it therefore has additional *moral* weight, that somehow the authority of the law is itself a moral ingredient that can tip the balance in favor of the law when there are moral considerations weighing against it. The mistake is encouraged by the notion that there are sources of *moral authority* that can operate independently of our personal moral resources and are in a position to nullify what conscience tells us is the right thing. When viewed in a spurious role as in itself a moral authority, the law becomes a major threat to the functioning of a sound moral life. The law must remain subject to the influence of our moral sensibilities rather than the political interests that are at the heart of legal authority. Laws are created by those who happen to possess political power, and they serve the interests and predilections of those in power as well as addressing more objectively those things of public interest that are brought to their attention. It was Bismarck who tellingly observed that two things no person should witness are how sausages and laws are made.

*   *   *

And yet we espouse *the rule of law as a moral ideal.* Surely this must mean that the law enjoys a certain moral preeminence. And so it does. It is the law when viewed as an authority that transcends the exercise of personal power – individual or collective – that represents a moral ideal. There are indefinitely many ways in which some of us can exercise power over others, and it is the law that keeps that exercise of power from being abused. And the red lines, the guidelines, the fences that the law provides to prevent abuse are grounded in our moral life. In a world in which some are strong and some are weak, we need the rule of law to keep the stronger from making victims of the weaker. Our moral life's concern for others depends on the rule of law to make that concern effective.

But the rule of law can itself become just what it is meant to prevent. Authority that exists to prevent the abuse of power can be power that abuses its power. It is more dangerous even than the naked abuse of power since it enjoys the trappings of legitimacy conferred on it by its acceptance as a social necessity. Instead of protecting the weak from abuse by the strong, the law can become an instrument of that abuse when it frees itself from the constraints of our moral life and instead makes itself available to those who seek to exploit others. Thus, the rule of law is a double-edged sword, able to serve our moral life or to undermine it.

* * *

I want now to make what may seem an extraordinary claim. The law, in its ideal form, is the crowning achievement of our moral life. And it is justice that is the jewel in the crown. In speaking of law in its ideal form I have in mind how the law is meant to be, what it professes as the right thing for itself, while at the same time acknowledging that in practice it often is corrupted and can fall well short of how it is mean to be.

Both in making and in applying law, satisfying the demands of justice is of paramount importance. And at the same time, justice is a constant presence in our moral consciousness. Sensitivity to injustice may not be the keenest of our moral sensitivities, with cruelty producing an even more shocking effect, but there is no moral misdemeanor that will torment our conscience with greater persistence than a case of injustice.

Concerns about justice in the law are intimately connected to more general concerns in our moral life. But justice is no single idea. There are six different sorts of moral concern in the law that can claim to be a concern with justice.

* * *

The first is justice as compassionate concern about the misfortunes inherent in the human condition. We are not all endowed with the same natural gifts, and some of us are put at a natural disadvantage by the handicaps that are our lot. Throughout our lives, we are liable to be struck down by illness, accidents, and natural disasters. Then there are the unhappy changes in our circumstances that occur when those on whom we rely are no longer willing or able to provide what we depend on for a decent life. Providing the help that is then needed is a claim on the conscience of the law. The law is able to address the needs of the needy better than any charity since it has at its disposal the collective resources of all of society. And the law preserves the dignity of those it helps by making the help it provides a matter of entitlement. It is an entitlement grounded in the moral mandate that we must not be indifferent to the suffering of others, and that minding one's own business is not a morally valid defense.

* * *

Though the programs created by law to help those in need may benefit individuals in the millions, it is ultimately the benefit that individuals enjoy as individuals that is the moral justification for imposing on a community the burden of helping those who need help. Being one's brother's keeper can assume immense proportions, and in doing so its moral foundation can become lost in the arena of political controversy where the law on which it depends must struggle to overcome objections. But however obscure the moral foundation may become, without that foundation the programs of help become opportunities for those who are in positions of power to use the collective resources to benefit themselves and their supporters.

* * *

Equality is a different kind of moral concern, and it is a second requirement marching under the banner of justice. Our moral life's most obvious concerns are helping those who need help; and more broadly, treating others as we wish to be treated ourselves. The great disparities in well-being that exist throughout society present a challenge to our moral sensitivities. Nature's unequal distribution of benefits and detriments results in natural inequalities. Treating others as one wishes to be treated oneself means lending a helping hand to those in a less fortunate position, just as one would wish to have a helping hand oneself if one needed it. It is impossible to do away with the inequalities; they are inherent in the human condition. But that is no excuse for ignoring them. Public policies that reduce both the inequalities themselves, as well as the effects of inequality, are a moral mandate for the law.

* * *

Equality in the law takes another form that calls for equal treatment of everyone who is involved in legal proceedings; a requirement that everyone must enjoy equal standing before the law is a third concern of justice. It is a requirement of justice that the differences among those subject to the law should not in any way influence the way the law is administered. Equal standing before and under the law means that the law gives no consideration to those things in life that generally make a difference in the way people treat one another. The law is a sanctuary in which the differences that make a difference generally are without their normal influence.

This ideal of the law, like all ideals, must face the challenges of a corrupting reality. Inevitably people with money who buy better legal services and make more extensive use of the law will have an advantage. This practical inequality under the law can to some extent be remedied by adhering in the administration of the law to the best reading of the law, a task that judges will always profess as their duty but will less often be a description of what they do. There is no reason why a poor man's case should be less persuasive when the controversy is with a rich man, except that the rich man will have the resources to prepare a stronger case. There is then a moral constraint, in the name of equality, for the legal system to exercise its ingenuity to ensure that the disparity in resources does not result in a disparity in justice.

* * *

Justice as fairness, is a fourth conception of justice in the law. It declares a union of ideas that are inseparable. Though fairness does not comprehend all that justice claims as its territory, there is no other moral sentiment that has as strong a claim to represent justice. Fairness in practice puts concerns about injustice to rest, and unfairness torments us in the name of injustice as long as we remain disposed to think about it.

The underlying moral concern is unequaled in importance. It is putting oneself in the position of another and claiming for oneself nothing that would not be acceptable to another. Ultimately, the appeal of fairness is not in a concern for others but rather a concern for oneself if one were in their position. The moral gist of fairness is putting oneself in the position of another and overcoming the barrier between oneself and others by exploiting a sense of a more comprehensive self.

* * *

Justice as due process is a fifth conception of justice that has a solid foundation in our moral life. Due process is a matter of the greatest importance in the law. It is indispensable if the law's position as the ultimate authority in society is not to lend itself to abuse. Due process ensures that the awesome powers the law possesses are exercised only in a way that respects the moral values reflected in basic human rights. Procedures are designed to protect those who are accused of wrongdoing or are in any other way liable to become the targets of claims by others. Due process is the assurance the law provides that in its operation it will itself remain above reproach. The kind of fairness one hopes for outside the law is a requirement imposed on itself by the law when it carries on its business.

It is something of a paradox that outside the law our moral life is carried on without the constraints of due process that the law requires. Our moral life is filled with a passionate exuberance in response to injustice, cruelty, dishonesty, and other varieties of moral deficiency. The restraint and circumspection required for due process is often lacking on such occasions. Our moral sensibilities are not designed to make sure we see the whole story, and we are often disposed to reach conclusions and pass judgment before everything that has a bearing has been considered. Even our initial position will often be determined by our predispositions rather than the facts that now present themselves. We are none of us anything like a court of law, with its stern disciplines that strive toward objectivity and the granting of opportunity for everything relevant to be considered. And so, it is the law that makes it possible for our moral life to have its fullest expression, free of the distraction and disorder borne of passion that is characteristic of our moral life when it is most engaged.

* * *

The justice that receives the most popular attention is criminal justice. It is also the most controversial. Punishment is the heart of the matter, and there are two opposing concerns.

Not letting people get away with their crimes seems an indispensable social necessity and at the same time a moral requirement. But how shall we prevent impunity in a way that is not morally disreputable? Inflicting harm and suffering to repay what victims of crime experience seems a morally inferior way to behave. It may pass muster as an all too human response, but ultimately it haunts us as an indictment of our better selves. Would a response that mixed the undesirable conditions of a restricted life with opportunities for improving oneself not be the morally right solution, a regime that seeks to remedy the defects, disabilities, and deficiencies that make criminal behavior more likely while at the same time leaving no room for a claim of impunity to flourish? From a moral perspective this means helping others who need our help, but without requiring of ourself a saintly acceptance of unrequited harm.

We can certainly be expected to relinquish vengefulness in any form as the morally correct public response to crime, though such private feelings are something to be countenanced as a natural exception to the moral elements in our make-up as human beings. It is an important feature of our life as social creatures that we allow the moral mandate to understand and help others to override the vengeful instincts that are our natural lot. The law is the most important social construct to achieve this taming of vengefulness in the name of moral probity, and it performs this miracle by making clear the criminal's need for help as well as the need for accountability.

Accountability is the broader concept of which criminal justice is one part. There are the many varieties of controversies that the law deals with as civil rather than criminal matters. Leaving people without a remedy for the non-criminal wrongs they suffer is a counterpart of impunity with even more baleful consequences since typically the loss suffered could be remedied by compensation. And once again the law comes to the rescue with justice rooted in a moral mandate. The law recognizes the wrongs that members of the community may suffer and provides the most appropriate means of remedying them. In civil matters accountability aims "to make the victim whole", and so more directly fulfills the moral mandate of helpfulness. In criminal proceedings there is only a measure of emotional satisfaction to the victim, which is a glaring moral deficiency. There are some attempts to provide material compensation to victims, as the Criminal Injuries Compensation Fund in Britain does, though the meager amount paid out after lengthy delays makes a mockery of the process and leaves criminal justice morally embarrassed.

* * *

The law is a repository for contention. Its mechanisms are welcoming places for the settlement of disputes that linger on when informal efforts to reconcile opposing positions have failed. And the law's development as a way to dispose of controversy has sharpened its moral sensibilities. To make the outcome of its proceedings seem as fair as the circumstances permit, the law makes use of our moral resources. Though we have different interests and take different views, as human beings in a common culture we share a common moral outlook. It is the law that allows our moral commonality to assert itself. Sequestered in our private affairs we are free to engage in moral self-indulgence. We see ourselves in a moral light that makes us right and others who oppose us wrong. The law forces a different perspective on us. Though we are not happy with an outcome adverse to our interests, if it is legally sound we are forced to accept it in good conscience. We can, of course, persist in a refusal to reconcile ourselves to what is decided even though the legal proceedings cannot in any way be faulted. There is always the possibility of moral perversity stepping in and taking charge. Our moral life, like all the rest of us, has its frailties.

* * *

Accountability for what we do depends to a great extent on just how involved we were in doing it. This is important when what we do results in something untoward occurring. Aiming to bring that about puts us in a different position than just acting with a measure of indifference or even simply not being careful enough in doing something that can be dangerous. In carrying on our daily lives, we are held accountable when things we do have untoward consequences, and when these things become the law's business they are scrutinized with exquisite care in order to assess liability fairly.

This moral underpinning of culpability shows itself more prominently in the careful discriminations that separate crimes of different degrees. But these legal definitions are not arbitrary legislative determinations. They are rooted in a moral mandate that says a person is accountable for the consequences of what he does according to what his role was in bringing them about.

* * *

A final thought is this. Without the law, our ability to make use of our moral resources would be severely curtailed. Without the law, we would be prevented from exercising freely our most basic rights and would be in constant danger of serious harm. To concern ourselves about others we must be secure ourselves and must live in conditions that are stable enough to allow what we do for others to have their expected benefit. It is a mistake to suppose that our moral life has a self-sufficiency that makes a nurturing environment unnecessary. Every human life depends on its own well-being for the moral life within it to flourish.

6

FOUR MORAL MISCHIEFS

We are accustomed to thinking of our moral life as a sunny walk in the uplands where we quite admirably resist temptations to do what is wrong, but also where we can seize opportunities to make the world a better place. And this is right. Our moral resources are devoted to making things better and to keeping things from being worse.

But our moral resources can also be misunderstood, abused, and used to bad effect. I want now to take note of four of the ways in which this happens.

Moral Personality

Our moral resources are equally available to all of us, but each of us has his or her own way of making use of those resources. In my book *Moral Mischief,* I sketched the various types of moral personality in which one finds that moral assets are misused or neglected, and I now offer an augmented reminder of these eccentricities. But before depicting what is abnormal, I must give some account of what I think is a morally healthy personality.

Paradoxically, its most striking feature is its lack of concern about moral matters. Good moral health is on display in how one carries on one's life, in what one does, not in what one professes. The *Admirable*

Amoralist, as I called him, does not concern himself with his own moral life, is never judgmental, never self-righteous, and is comfortable recognizing the foibles in himself and in others that are part of the human condition. His lack of constant critical concern about conduct attests to his moral soundness. But there is more.

When there is good reason not to tell the truth he has no qualms about avoiding needless embarrassment. Circumstances sometimes make a declaration of the truth an embarrassing indiscretion and the *Admirable Amoralist* recognizes that there is a time and a place for truth-telling. Honesty is truth's sibling, and it is similarly subject to a discretion imposed on it by the occasion, when honesty can be too painful and discretion dictates that it be sacrificed for a harmless fudge. His responsible exercise of supervening discretion is this man's most distinctive feature. Those familiar with the term will call him a *Mensch*.

The *Admirable Amoralist* stands in stark contrast to what I have called the *Moral Idiot Savant*. He keeps every promise he has made no matter how foolish it appears in the light of day, and can always be relied on to tell the truth, the whole truth, and nothing but the truth no matter what the consequences may be. The *Moral Idiot Savant* may seem to be hopelessly infatuated with moral mandates. But in fact, he is more likely to be driven by a morbid fear of doing wrong. His moral fastidiousness is a good reason for others to give him a wide berth.

Some people profess to see only the good in others. This is a good thing when it leads to a reform of criminal justice that emphasizes rehabilitation rather than retribution, and more generally when it encourages helping others to overcome their shortcomings rather than simply condemning them for their wrongdoing. But there are people we might call *Moral Polyannas* who refuse to see what is plainly morally wrong for what it is and instead put a benign face on what deserves to be called to account. This denial of moral accountability, which is a suspension of moral judgment, can easily leave our moral life out of kilter when there are legitimate grievances seeking the satisfaction that justice provides.

Next, there is the *Immoralist*. He thinks moral concerns are for weaker people. The *Immoralist* has a regard for himself and for whatever interests him that overrides concern for others. Fulfilling his ambitions and satisfying whatever desires he has take precedence over everything else. There are many laws that protect against dishonesty and prohibit deception. These laws are moral mandates that have teeth and simply ignoring such laws would be imprudent, so the *Immoralist* will seek to find ways around such laws when they stand in his way. But it is the teeth, and not moral suasion, that influences him in what he does. Such people are much admired for their accomplishments, with the moral stains along the way regarded as the regrettable price that must be paid for the rich rewards. Trophies of wealth and power compel greater admiration than displays of moral excellence.

Less extreme in his indifference to moral rules is the *Fickle Moralist*. He is sensitive to the views that others might have of him, but does not feel that moral concerns in themselves are a good enough reason to alter his conduct when morally questionable means are the most efficient way of achieving something he desires. So, he is careful about appearances, availing himself of whatever cosmetic opportunities there might be to avoid giving moral offense, but without any moral conviction.

The *Dedicated Moralist* occupies an opposite position. He thinks moral questions are of paramount importance no matter what other concerns there may be. There is an assumption that human nature is fundamentally flawed and in constant need of moral supervision. Moral authority of one sort or another is thought to be a *sine qua non* of our moral life, and purely practical considerations must always take a back seat when moral judgments are to be made.

More extreme still is the *Moral Enthusiast*. Anything that lends itself to criticism of any sort will be turned into an occasion for blaming and shaming, with condemnation and stigmatization never far behind. The *Moral Enthusiast* pre-empts the forum, and constructive measures directed to remedy and improvement are neglected. This will often be a welcome development for those who would otherwise have to foot the bill to set things right. It is moral criticism employed to defeat morally enlightened policy.

Finally, there is the *Moral Bully*. He turns our moral life against itself by demanding conformity in the name of some authority. The authority bedecks itself with the trappings of Morality, which, as we know from previous discussion, derives its strength not from the moral excellence of what it has to say, but from the mechanisms of enforcement that it has at its disposal. The moral claims of Fascism or Communism are rooted in a totalitarian Morality that eulogizes group interests and disparages individual values. Religions likewise give the arbitrary edicts of a divine authority a standing as Morality just because of the incontestable authority from which they emanate. And in a family once again there is a kind of Morality that attaches to what those in authority say just because of their status. The arbitrary exercise of authority under the guise of Morality leads to moral brutalism, which is the will of those in authority being given recognition as morally correct, regardless of what sound moral judgment might have to say.

Thought Experiments

One of the many remarkable things about the human mind is its ability to imagine situations that might well exist but cannot actually be found anywhere in the real world. It is a God-like power, an ability to appropriate selectively from reality and while remaining true to reality make use of this new construction for whatever purpose one might have in mind. This gives people who are happy to exercise their ingenuity the opportunity to raise questions about what is right and what is wrong with reference to particular conduct, *but in the abstract*, free from the inconvenience of further questions that common sense would like answered. Thought experiments are devised with a dedication to preserving this purity. Dilemmas about who shall live and who shall die are presented for our consideration, and they admit of no escape from the anguish of the moment when a decision must be made.

Undoubtedly, thought experiments' most popular moral dilemma concerns a runaway trolley which is certain to kill five people who are tied to the track unless the trolley is diverted onto a spur track, where there is only one person tied to the track. In one telling it is the driver who must choose, in another it is someone standing next to a switch that would divert the trolley.

But there is an interesting embellishment.

There is a footbridge under which the trolley must pass. Leaning over the rail as he watches the trolley hurtling out of control is a fat man. If he is pushed over the rail onto the tracks his bulk will stop the trolley and save the lives of the hapless five. The dilemma now is whether to sacrifice the fat man to save five lives, one life lost but five lives saved from certain death.

This dilemma was featured in a book whose title was *Would You Kill the Fat Man? The Trolley Problem and What Your Answer Tells Us About Right and Wrong*, published in 2014 and bearing the distinguished imprint of Princeton University Press. The killing of the fat man was not advocated by the author, but as the title of the book indicates, the possibility of killing him was given serious consideration. This testing of right and wrong in the imagination has much to tell us about such thought experiments generally.

The first thing to notice is that killing the fat man is murder, cold-blooded and wanton. Just imagine someone charged with his murder pleading that he was justified in what he did because it saved five lives. He would, if lucky, be deemed mentally ill and a danger to the public if left free to kill others when he believed their death might save other lives. Taking this thought experiment seriously involves a selective disregard of what is certain to happen as a result of what is done, and especially the legal consequences.

This suggests what is a fatal flaw in such thought experiments. Our moral sensibilities have shaped the law, and it is in the law that we have procedures for deciding how to deal with such moral dilemmas. For one thing, the law wants to know a great deal more than thought experiments wish to tell us. Instead of taking a God's-eye snapshot and asking what should be done, the law concerns itself with liability, criminal and civil, and asks the kinds of questions that help in assigning blame or that tend to exculpate. The law asks questions whose answers implicate our moral sensibilities and in the end, produce moral judgments that reflect the complexity of the real world. Thought experiments, on the other hand, are meant to be unyieldingly stark. We would like to know what in the world people are doing tied to trolley tracks. Exactly what do the trolley driver and the bystander really know? And there are a great many other questions affecting the liability of various parties lurking in the background. In insisting on maintaining its arbitrary simplification, the thought experiment deprives our moral life of the ability to bring the full force of its resources into play.

And it is a mistake to suppose that every moral dilemma can be resolved in a moral judgment. In the trolley story, the people who can make the decision about who shall live and who shall die are not in a position to make a morally informed choice because the pressure of their circumstances deprive them of resort to their moral resources, and so their conduct is no longer subject to moral judgment. The law, for its part, is similarly handicapped by this inability of the targeted people to make a moral judgment, and may consider only claims of civil, but not criminal, liability since there are legal principles other than those relating to personal conduct that the law can employ. And this confession of moral inadequacy by the law should be imitated by moral theorists. A God's-eye snapshot cannot yield what is needed for sound moral judgment of right and wrong from us mere mortals.

So, let's be clear.

The thought experiment seeks a moral judgment about conduct. But it is unclear about whose moral judgment is being sought. Is it the moral judgment of the person who controls the destiny of the trolley, or is it the moral judgment of those who are concerned to pass judgment on that person's conduct?

The person who determines the destiny of the trolley is in no condition to arrive at a moral judgment. In the desperate circumstances in which he finds himself he is effectively deprived of the use of his personal moral resources. We cannot expect him to consider whatever is necessary for moral choice any more than we could expect him to meet an intellectual challenge requiring reflective consideration.

The rest of us can certainly make use of our moral resources but, alas, the thought experiment has put its hermetic seal on the facts that are provided, and this has deprived us of the further information that is necessary to render a moral judgment. In any case, that judgment is the kind of judgment that would guide the law in dealing with the situation presented by the thought experiment. It is a judgment about liabilities, not about right and wrong. And such a judgment is the only way of dealing with the dilemma in a morally sound way.

Thought experiments are best viewed as fun, a folly and a form of moral alchemy that is a diversion from the serious business of moral philosophy.

Other Minds

Nothing in our moral life is more distinctive than its concern with how we treat one another. And of course, it is persons in all their baffling complexity that are the object of this concern. People are part of the world that we have easy access to. We are curious about someone and know how to get to know whatever we wish to know about him. Of course, a great deal might remain unknown, but even then, just as it is with the rest of the world, we know what it is that we don't know. People are social creatures, and as such develop in ways that facilitate their getting to know one another.

Other minds are a very different story. Unlike other persons, other minds are largely a mystery. And this is not surprising considering how uncertain we are about our own mind. Though we have privileged access to our own mind it is far from clear what really goes on there. It is the outside world that all of us share which has the stability and the clarity that allows it to be known with certainty. Our minds, however, for all their intimacy, are known to us much less certainly. Our minds are mainly a fleeting process rather than a fixed object, and compounding the difficulty, the process is inherently vague. Our minds, unlike our bodies, are full of novelties that come as surprises, which adds to our sense of uncertainty.

Still, we do have an awareness of what goes on in our minds, unsettled and incomplete though it may be. Other minds are another story. For acquaintance with what goes on in other minds, we are at the mercy of the person whose mind it is. What people think and feel remains their own undisclosed business until they choose to tell us about it, or more often, till they say or do things that make clear what they are thinking or feeling. And since we are massively dependent on others in every aspect of our life, we are naturally curious about what is going on in the minds of those whose cooperation we depend on as well as those who may do things that harm us or in some other way displease us.

* * *

The inscrutability of other minds creates a breeding ground for suspicions. We are concerned that those we depend on leave us feeling comfortable about them, yet we are aware that others have interests that do not sit comfortably with our own. Lovers' anxieties can take this to a fevered pitch, and just within a family suspicions of a husband's or wife's infidelity are fostered by the inability of each of them to see what's going on in the mind of the other. Suspicions are a constant feature in the affairs of the great world. What political leaders say is often not what they think and can even be intended to mislead. What others are really up to is a concern in business, as it is in international affairs. And since reading minds is not possible there is a constant need to discover whatever one can that has been disclosed but is being kept secret.

Suspicion has an impact on our moral life. When people have convinced themselves that others are harboring thoughts and feelings that are inimical to them they act to protect themselves. The First World War, a moral depravity and a tragedy on the grandest scale, might well likely not have taken place if what was really going on in the minds of each nation's leaders was known to all of the others.

* * *

One of suspicion's most daunting moral menaces is conspiracy theories. When something bad occurs we seek an explanation. This offers an opportunity for malign interests to suggest that someone or something they wish to denigrate was the cause. Sinister motives always have greater appeal to the imagination than hard facts, and what the imagination in its turn produces is more alluring than the dreary reliability of common sense with its tedious insistence on plausibility. And so there is always a ready audience for whatever mischief the conspiracy theorist has in mind. Ultimately it is the suspicion aroused by the inscrutability of other minds that sustains the conspiracy theory in spite of its implausibility.

* * *

The inscrutability of other minds gives us a convenient excuse for not giving recognition to morally significant changes that take place in people. People who commit crimes bear a stigma that prevents them from redeeming themselves in the eyes of others, and the inward change that has taken place in them remains inaccessible to others. Outward changes are often insufficient, at least in the short term, to convince others of the inward changes that have taken place. Sincerely declaring that one sees things very differently now is all too likely to meet with skepticism and the thought that "he would say that, wouldn't he".

And there are other reasons for another's inward change remaining unrecognized. It is more convenient to cherish and defend an opinion one has become comfortable with than it is to change one's mind and have the burden of explaining why. Changing one's mind about something of importance is often a matter of *amour propre*, touching on self-respect and even vanity. When it comes to changing one's mind about a person one is spared this embarrassment by the inscrutability of what really is going on inside another person's mind; and so, sadly, one sticks to one's wrong opinion, with moral reconciliation now impossible.

* * *

The inscrutability of other minds is exploited by attributing sinister origins to what is expressed. This results in a better-safe-than-sorry policy directed to the regulation of free expression.

Language itself endows us with an abundant capacity to hurt others, whether by casual insult, or by virulent expression of hatred. And there are also intermediate forms of incivility – from good-natured jokes at another's expense to humiliating ridicule. The animus in all of these is to be found wholly in what is said, without any suggestion of something unsaid that remains hidden in the mind of the speaker.

But there are more sinister expressions that are thought to be like the visible part of an iceberg whose undisclosed portion remains in the mind of the speaker, inaccessible and beyond our reach. The hidden material is hostile, or in some other way disreputable, and it is the mission of an alert and enlightened speech police to protect us from it.

There are first of all the strictures of those in authority who are concerned not to allow hidden defections from a prevailing orthodoxy. In modern times this is found most frequently in the thought police of totalitarian societies, though some religions are still concerned that minds remain uncorrupted by unacceptable notions.

A far less authoritarian orthodoxy exists in the form of political correctness, where wrong thinking is discouraged by a reform of various expressions. A "pet" becomes an "animal household companion", and so one's mind is purged of attitudes of species superiority. It is a sanitizing of the mind, where, if neglected, unwholesome thoughts and feelings express themselves covertly through commonplace use of infected terms.

Then there are the undetectable demons of the mind. There may be no evidence of them but what is known about a person makes it virtually certain that they exist in his mind. Recent concern about micro-aggressions is a splendid example. A teacher's background ensures that he harbors prejudices that he may well be unconscious of himself; however, some of his words can confidently be assumed to contain some indication of those prejudices, though admittedly they fail to qualify as evidence of them. But of course, no one would want to provide evidence of his prejudice, and the fact that he provides none confirms that he is hiding his prejudices.

Here we have the inscrutability of another's mind used to condemn him, and since there is no evidence, there can be no defense. It is an exquisite exploitation of the predicament of other minds.

The Quest for Moral Certainty

Moral certainty is a persistent concern. When we have the assurance that our moral judgment is right, we feel a deep satisfaction; and we do not happily accept suggestions that we have got it wrong. But our quest for certainty goes beyond our conclusion here and now, a reassurance that it deserves to win the current argument. In serious matters, we want to know that our judgment is unimpeachable, *a moral truth,* and not just a convenient piece of moral expediency. The same question might be decided differently at some time in the past, or even now in some other place, at home or abroad, and we want to know that what we decide has a certainty that assures it will prevail as the truth wherever and whenever. The truth is it is always morally wrong to enslave another person, and that's an end to it.

* * *

There is *something personal* about moral judgment that makes it more compelling than our decisions about matters of fact, and this is so even when we do not have a personal stake in the controversy. Our moral life is an integral part of our sense of ourself. What it comprehends is something we care about as part of the person we are, and so we have stronger feelings about it than we do about things that are unconnected to us, however intriguing they may be.

(It is true we take positions on many different sorts of controversial questions, and we regard our opinion as entitled to be respected as part of the respect we ourselves are entitled to. And there are also things to which we are affiliated – religious, national, ethnic – that are so much a part of our identity that if they are slighted we take umbrage personally. Our serious moral judgments, however, are embedded in personal conviction, which give them a heightened sensitivity, more like a toothache than a headache.)

And here we encounter a paradox. To confer the mantle of certainty on moral judgments we must be satisfied that they are *objective*. If they are just an expression of how we feel, of what we think is right, they cannot claim certainty, which consists of their being right no matter how we might feel, or what we might think. Our moral judgments may be experienced deeply, but if they are morally certain they cannot depend for their certainty simply on the strength of our commitment to them.

But what is it that we are really seeking when we seek moral certainty?

Objectivity is the catchword. This is meant to suggest that the mind simply apprehends but does not contribute to what is apprehended. The truth is there for anyone to see, and it is unaffected by how we might feel about what is there to be seen. The earth is not flat, and it is wrong to torture babies. Both are true no matter what anyone might say.

There is a problem. Moral truths have their own home in our sensibilities. And our sensibilities are a *subjective*, not an objective, phenomenon. They belong to the person who is making the moral judgment, and in fact play the most important part in arriving at a moral judgment. Aren't we then prevented from claiming objectivity for moral judgments?

The objectivity that we require is found in the sensibilities that make it possible for us to carry on our moral lives in a moral community. There is certainty about torturing babies being morally wrong because of the uniformity of sensibility about that in our moral community. Moral judgments that rely on sensibilities not enjoying the consensus of a moral community do not, unfortunately, enjoy the blessings of certainty. But there is hope. As our sensibilities mature, individually and collectively, we become better people, and our moral judgments have greater certainty. In the meantime, we can take comfort in the great consensus regarding the most egregious moral wrongs, though it must be said that what is practiced does not always conform to what is preached.

I end with a caveat. Morality depends for acceptance of its pronouncements on some external authority rather than the sensibilities that constitute our internal moral life. Morality will always claim certainty for its moral pronouncements. A failure to claim certainty would undermine its authority. But of course, its certitude is *faux* certainty; and only when Morality espouses the messages of our sensibilities can it aspire to certainty.

Printed in Great Britain
by Amazon

0451aa1a-b738-4852-a295-c32f681d6e09R01